What to Exp... When Mommy's Having a Baby

Heidi Murkoff

Illustrated by Laura Rader

HarperFestival®
A Division of HarperCollinsPublishers

Just Ask Angus

Hello! My name is Angus. Some people call me the Answer Dog, because I like to answer all kinds of questions about growing up. It's good to ask questions because what you know, helps you grow!

Are you ready to find out what to expect when your mommy's having a baby, and what you can do to help? Then let's get started! Follow me. . . .

Your friend,

Angus

Where is the baby?

The baby is in a special place in your mommy's belly called a uterus. Some people say womb instead of uterus. The uterus is a warm, cozy, snuggly place, the very best place for a baby to grow.

Curl up in a little ball, and wrap yourself in a warm blanket. Now you know how it feels to be a baby inside a uterus!

Uterus or Womb

How did the baby get in there?

Your mommy and daddy love each other a lot, and they also love you. Together, you make a family. Being a family is so special that your mommy and daddy decided to make another baby. Making a baby is like putting pieces of a puzzle together. Mommies have one piece, called an ovum. Daddies have the other piece, called sperm. When a mommy and daddy want to make a baby, the daddy puts his sperm inside the mommy. The daddy's sperm fits together with the mommy's ovum. Then a baby starts growing.

Believe it or not, you were once a tiny baby growing inside your mommy's uterus. Ask to see pictures of your mommy when she was pregnant with you.

How can a baby fit inside Mommy?

A baby doesn't start out baby-size. In the beginning, the baby is smaller than a pea, and your mommy's belly looks the same as always. But just like you, the baby grows a little bit every day. And as it grows bigger . . . and bigger . . . and bigger . . . so does your mommy's belly!

When you were inside your mommy's uterus, you were tiny like a pea, too. Look at a pea. Now look at yourself in the mirror. See how much you've grown!

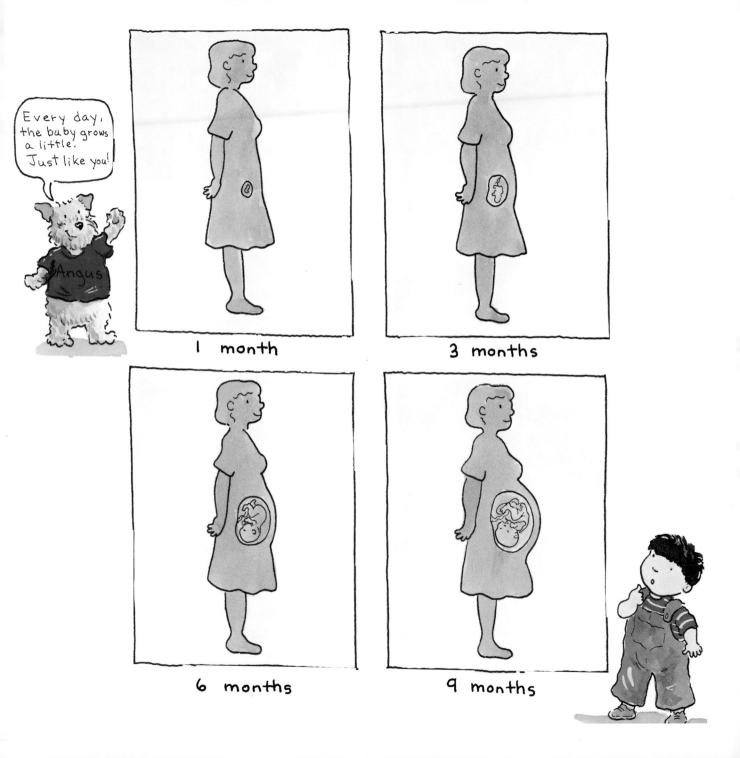

What makes the baby grow? How can I help?

Since the baby is growing inside of Mommy, she helps it grow the most. But you and Daddy can also help. You can eat healthy foods with Mommy. You can take walks together. You can take your vitamins together. You can make sure you all get plenty of rest. And since these things help you grow, too, you and the baby will be growing at the same time!

What's your favorite healthy food? Can you guess what mine is?

How does the baby eat?

hile the baby is inside your mommy's uterus, it can't eat the way you do. But it still needs food, so your mommy shares the food she eats with the baby. Inside your mommy, the food she eats changes into food that's right for the baby (babies aren't ready to eat pizza yet!). A special tube called the umbilical cord sends the food right to the baby's belly. Once the baby is born, it will eat through its mouth. Guess what happens to the umbilical cord? It becomes a belly button!

Where is your belly button? Can you believe you used to get your food through there?

Can the baby hear and see me?

The baby can hear a lot of what's going on outside your mommy's belly. It can hear your daddy reading you a story, it can hear the music your mommy is playing, and, it can even hear you talking. That helps the baby get to know you even before it's born. The baby's eyes are open sometimes, but it can't see through the uterus. That's okay, because when the baby is born it will have lots and lots to look at—especially you!

Babies love to listen to singing. Try putting your mouth really close to your mommy's belly. Then sing your favorite song to the baby.

What does the baby do all day?

The baby does a lot of the same things that babies do after they're born. It sleeps a lot. It eats. It sucks its thumb. It wiggles around. It yawns. Sometimes it even gets the hiccups. When the baby's the size of a pea, your mommy can't feel the baby moving around. But when the baby gets bigger, she can feel it a lot. You may be able to feel the baby kicking, too, if you put your hand on your mommy's belly!

Babies like to be touched, even when they're inside their mommies. Ask your mommy if you can rub her belly gently. I bet the baby will like that!

When the baby gets bigger you can feel it move!

A baby eats...

... gets the hiccups...

... and sucks its thumb!

It sleeps a lot!

Why doesn't Mommy feel well sometimes?

Helping a baby grow is hard work. Sometimes your mommy may get tired, or her back may hurt, or she may get a tummy ache. Sometimes she may feel like eating everything in sight! But that doesn't mean that she's sick—it just means that she's pregnant.

Next time your mommy doesn't feel well, maybe you can bring her a pillow, and you can lie down together.

Why does Mommy go to the doctor so much?

These visits to the doctor are checkups for the baby. They're a lot like the checkups you have. The doctor weighs your mommy and touches and measures her belly to see how much the baby has grown. Next, the doctor listens to the baby's heartbeat. Maybe you can listen to it, too.

Many times, families don't know if the baby is a boy or a girl until it's born. But it's fun to guess!

When will the baby come out? How does it get out?

Babies stay in the uterus until they're big enough to be born. That usually takes about nine months, which is a pretty long time. When the baby is ready to come out, it starts moving down a tunnel called a birth canal. When it gets to the bottom of the birth canal, the baby comes out of an opening between Mommy's legs called the vagina. Your mommy and daddy will probably go to the hospital for the baby to be born, so the doctor can help. And as soon as the baby is born, guess who's a big brother or sister? You are!

Ask your mommy to show you pictures of you on the day you were born. Can you believe you were ever that little?

A Word to Parents

Congratulations—you're having another baby. You're thrilled, you're excited, you're a little nervous (will two be twice the fun, or twice the work?)—but most of all, you're wondering how you're going to explain this miraculous but extremely complex process to your older, but still very young, child.

What to Expect When Mommy's Having a Baby is a good place to begin. It isn't meant to anticipate or completely answer all of your child's questions. Rather, it's meant to give voice to some of the questions your child may have (but may not be able to clearly express) and to serve as a jumping-off point for further discussion and dialogue about how a baby is created, how it grows, and ultimately, how it comes out to join the family.

How much information is not enough? How much is too much? For that, as always, let your child be your guide. I suggest you read through the book first, so that you'll be familiar enough with the content that you can mentally add or edit as you read it to your child. The key to answering a child's questions—particularly about subjects like reproduction and the human body—is to give as much information as is requested, but no more. Keep your explanations honest, straightforward, and accurate, but geared to your child's level of comprehension. Most of all, try hard (and it will be hard!) not to appear shocked, embarrassed, or disapproving when your child broaches subjects that may be uncomfortable for you. Remember, a young child's curiosity about everything in his or her environment is natural. By encouraging curiosity, you'll nurture a love of learning that will last a lifetime.